Easy Ways to

Make Money Online

Find Out How to Make an Income on the Internet

By: Kaye Dennan

ISBN-13 978-1492947707

Table of Contents

PUBLISHERS NOTES

Disclaimer

Paperback Edition

Manufactured in the United States of America

DEDICATION

I would like to take this opportunity to thank all the trainers I have had over the years who have helped me master making money online.

INTRODUCTION

When I decided to write this book I really found it difficult to know where to start because there are so many myths floating around about 'making money online', some of them true and some of them would equate to handful of fluff.

Let me say that it most definitely is possible to make money online.

The purpose of this book is to enlighten you as to some simple but effective ways to make money online within a range of elemental website techniques.

But what does need to be remembered is that each and every year, in fact each and every month, there are more and more first time online entrepreneurs trying to make money online. That is the downside, but on the upside there are so many ways to make money online that many are wide open for beginners.

Because of the fact that there are so many ways to make money online I have focused this book on enlightening people who do not have too many technical skills how they can start to make money online.

The fact that you do not have many computer skills or internet knowledge does not mean you cannot succeed in your endeavors, but merely means that it may take you longer at the start and you most definitely will need to be involved in training in your chosen field.

Any trainer worth their salt will tell you though, that earning money online is not something that will happen overnight. For example, you will hear many people say that they have made all sorts of money on eBay, but if you delve further into their history you will find that most have had a shop for something like 6-8 years, starting when eBay was relatively new and with thousands less 'shopkeepers' than there are today. But that does not mean that you should not do that. What it does mean is that you need to learn how to do it the right way from eBay gurus, people who have been making money on eBay for some time.

It is the people who have been around the various money earning sites for a number of years that have learned the hard way. They have had to try and test things themselves as there were no trainers in the early days of making money online. In most cases these people have learned hundreds of tips that if you learn them too, will help you get the success you are after far quicker than they ever did.

You might say, 'but why would they show us?' Quite simply the reason is that they are not threatened by you. These trainers are so established in their niche that they do not fear newcomers. They have a following that they keep in touch with and they know how to monetize their list. They are also aware just how big the market place is and that given their consistency will continue to make the money they desire.

The success of making money online comes with building a database of satisfied customers and building a good reputation. When you have those you just can't go wrong. It is the building of the database of customers that will take the time and effort. Then you must keep in touch with all your past customers and contacts on a regular basis.

That is the real essence of having a successful business online.

QUESTIONS ABOUT MAKING MONEY ONLINE

At this very point you need to understand that if you truly want to make money online you are going to have to put in the hard work. It's a bummer, I know, but then this is the real world.

You have heard the expression, **"The harder I work the luckier I get!"**

Well, that is what it is all about. Hard work! Especially in the beginning!

Making money in any way shape or form takes hard work, not just on the internet. Those who make money online regard their activities as their 'business'. It is having a business mindset that sets them apart from those that just dabble with making money and who give up within a few weeks because they are not seeing results. When you start out online it could well be a few months before you see any return on your results.

Making money on the internet is a numbers game. You have to get the numbers to get the sales or the work, whatever it is that you choose to go after.

There is no way you will make money unless you put in the hard work, the long hours and make a commitment to work at it each and every day. The thing is, when you have put in the hard yards so to speak, there will come a time when you will be able to cut back your hours as you will learn quicker techniques and learn how to automate more and more of your business.

But the questions you need to ask yourself before you go down this path are:

- How much money can I make
- How much money do I want to make
- How much money do I need to make
- How much money can I invest in growing a business online
- How much time do I have to put into a business online
- What skills have I got
- What skills will I need

There are thousands of knowledgeable people who are online who want to share their knowledge and if you are serious about earning money online then you will at some stage most likely have to get involved in some courses that will equip you properly for what you want to do.

In saying that, I will say right at the very beginning, "do read between the lines when you are reading sales letters." When you first start out and until you get to know some of the creditable people selling their services, make sure that you are paying through a creditable payment gateway and that they give a guarantee of refund. Paypal.com, Productpay.com and Clickbank.com are a few of the payment gateways that have a good reputation. Most of the creditable trainers give a guarantee with their training whereby you get a period of time to get a refund if you are not happy with what you are getting.

As you get to know the various trainers you will most likely pay for their services through their own particular payment methods.

When I first started out online 7 years ago I paid $5,000 and joined up with a publishing group. On the face of it the whole set up was a great idea and there was good support, but not knowing anything about what was required online I did not realize that with all the information that was available to me there was very little 'how to' instruction. Sure we were told what to do, which all sounded good, but we were not told 'how' to do it and that in itself is a big difference. For people who have not done anything like that before it needs much more than being told what to do, it needed instruction on exactly how to do it.

Today there are really brilliant trainers and web-based training companies who not only provide PDF documents but detailed video training as well. I will list a number of these in my Appendices so that you will at least get some reputable contacts to start with. I will only mention people I have worked with and who I would happily use again.

A good place to start finding out more about these people is to find and follow them on Facebook and then you will see what others have to say.

Answers to the Questions Above

How much money can I make?

There is no doubt that there are very, very successful online entrepreneurs who have made millions. Many of them, as I mentioned before, started out quite a few years ago, but some only started about 5 or so years ago. How much money you can make will depend on what way you decide to make money, what resources you have behind you to get your business off the ground and how much time you have to spend on it?

If you are going to go down the path of selling your services for a $ return on time, such as writing articles, graphic design, etc. then you will be limited as there is only so much time you can work in a week. (Nothing wrong with this at all, I am just saying.) When you become an expert in that field you can demand quite a large sum of monies for your expertise.

But if you decide to go down the path where you can use a service like Amazon and Ebay where you can sell hundreds of times to hundreds of people then you have a much better chance of making big money in the end, even if it does take you some months or even years to get the ultimate result you want.

On the other hand you may have already been dabbling with Ebay but not being successful. Just by getting some expert training may change all of that for you.

In the end 'how much money you make' will depend on the three basics mentioned above: system, resources and time.

How much money do I want to make?

To answer this question it again relates back to what I was just talking about in the previous chapter. What you can make and want to make, need to be worked out from the same perspective.

Be realistic with deciding what you want. It is most unlikely that you will make much money initially as you go through your learning curve and for this reason many people start their online business while they are still working offline.

Or alternatively, you may start writing for set $, to keep a small income flow but also start building your business into a bigger money making machine using the techniques where you can get big numbers for your products or services that you sell.

Alternatively you may have the resources to jump straight in after you have done your research and found out what system you want to be involved in.

How much money do I need to make?

This is probably not too difficult to work out as you know your living expenses and knowing this figure will help you decide if you need to stay employed while you start online or start with a small stable income doing the work for $ jobs while you build another online business.

OR you may have the time and resources to go without income for a bit while you go through the learning curve. Only you can answer that.

How much money do I need to invest in growing a business online?

I would love to convincingly say that you can make money online without investing any of your own money in your business, but the reality is that if you do not invest your money in yourself to learn from the experts your income growth will be anything from nothing to very slow. For example, if you were doing work for $ and working through an outsourcing site then you don't need any money at all.

You can start with next to nothing with some of the ideas we talk about in this book, but if you want to be autonomous, build your own websites and do marketing you will need some funds behind you.

If you don't have some money behind you it will be more difficult to get the good advice and training you need. Plus, when building websites and such like, you do need to be buying royalty free photos, join data processing sites for your emails and such like. None of them cost lots of money on their own, but it does all add up.

You don't necessarily need thousands and thousands of dollars, but it would help to have a couple of thousand dollars accessible over a period of time for you to use if you need to.

All the good trainers give away a certain amount of good information for free, but you will find that you want to buy ebooks and courses which could be anything from $30 to $600, or even more (although you probably won't spend more in the early stages.)

I personally am looking at a course at the moment that will cost me $4,000. Not an amount to be sneezed at.

How much time do I have to put into a business online?

The time you have to put into your business will relate, to an extent, to the amount you can make. In saying that, don't think that just because you put in 30 hours a week you are going to make money. If you don't do things the right way you may not make anything.

Then again you could have a really good system and earn several thousand a month within 6 months or so. Either way you are going to have to put in a good amount of time to get your venture off the ground.

If you choose to do something a little more technical you may have such a big learning curve that initially you spend more time learning than you do actually working on your business to make money. That is alright as long as it sits within your plan.

What skills have I got?

Obviously working online means you are going to have to have some computer skills. In saying that, when I started on the internet 7 years ago, I did not even have an email and could barely put a letter together and print it out, but I really wanted to have an online business so I was prepared to do whatever it took to make it happen. The one advantage I did have was that I am a quick touch typist.

I can now build websites (I have over 30), I write ebooks and have more than 14 of those in the market place at the moment with more on the way. I have written ebooks for clients and I write blogs for several clients. I am now starting to build a portfolio of affiliate sites.

This is how you too can build your business if you choose to. You can see that what I have done is have several income sources: my own websites, affiliate sales, selling ebooks online and writing for clients.

So when it comes down to it, it is not what you can do, but what you are prepared to do!

You may start out small not knowing exactly what you want to do, but at least learning computer skills and as time goes by find what it is that you really want to concentrate on and what you really enjoy.

After going round in circles for a while, following different trainings that I took, looking at coaching and other ideas, I have finally found my niche and that is writing books. It would have been the furthest thought from my mind when I started out working on the internet 7 years ago. In fact, it was because I had to write articles for my websites that my interest in writing developed.

You know though, the funniest thing was, when I had my first website (the one I referred to I bought for $5,000) I didn't even know what at article was and of everything else I had to do to work the website writing articles was the one thing that brought me to tears. I absolutely froze at the idea of putting an article together. But what was even funnier was the fact that after I had written a few, I realized that I had in fact been writing for years and years as I had always written all our advertising and marketing matter in our small businesses.

So, it just goes to show, give something a name you are a not familiar with and it can freak you out!

What skills will I need?

When starting out there is a lot to learn so try to keep your focus on just one or two things at a time. Learn those well and then move on to the next thing. From the ideas I list further on there may be several possibilities that interest you.

One of the hardest things to do if you want to work full-time at making money online, as I did, is to keep focused on the one method of doing so. As you spread your wings further and further, and follow more and more trainers and online chatter, you will come across more and more ways to earn that sound exciting and it is hard not to jump from one to the other.

I know I did jump from one to the other for years until the end of last year when I felt I had found my forte in writing. My two loves are writing and building websites.

You will find your way and like me, and possibly have several things going at the same time. Most people do, but learn one well if you want to stay with that method, before moving on to the next one. When you do take on several methods of making money online you need to ensure that you keep up the marketing of anything you want to keep active so that you do not lose the momentum you have built up.

You will realize as you read through the following pages that you most likely do have skills that you can use to build a business in some of the areas mentioned. Then again you may want to do something entirely different from what you have been doing in the past.

Outsourcing

As you get more experienced you will realize that organization is the key to doing the business you want to do. If your business grows to the extent that you are making money and yet do not have enough time in the day to do all you need to do, then you may need to look at outsourcing some of your work. Depending on what you need done given the time and experience you have, you may just get articles written for your blogs, or you may contract someone to do your marketing. That will all fall into place in time as you grow.

When outsourcing work you can start with spending just a few dollars a week and as you build your business you can get more and more work done. Eventually you may even get to the stage of having someone work for you several hours a week. Employing a Virtual Assistant (VA) to help you and whom you can train to do what you need done.

Also it is quite comforting to know that with whatever help you do need there are very skilled people available to support you.

In the next chapters I will explain some of the easier ways to make money online.

FREELANCING/PAY-PER-PROJECT

This is one of the easiest ways to make money online, is a very popular and lucrative way for people to start earning from working online.

If you have skills that others can use then you can be a provider to others. There is a wide range of skills that are in demand through this type of business and to name a few there are:

- Design and multimedia
- Article writing
- Ebooks and blogs
- Translation
- Sales and marketing
- Finance and management
- IT and programming
- Social media posting

Earning money from writing for others who have selling sites, blog sites or information based products is one of the easiest ways to make money online. You will need to have reasonably good writing skills and an understanding of what is required by those people ordering your services. People ask for articles on a wide range of topics.

If you are conversant with several languages and can transcribe then this can be a very good source for you as more and more people are placing their products into the market place in several languages.

You will need to have the knowledge of using the right keywords, to be able to place them in the right places and know how to present good articles, blogs or books, so that you continue to get good reviews and recommendations. That is what you need to focus on.

You could also transcribe from audio and write reviews.

When starting out on these sites you need to complete your profile properly, have samples of your work in your profile and for the first few jobs you would probably need to bid quite low to get the work and then start getting good reviews. Then when you have a following you could slowly increase your prices. You would have to gauge that by the work you get.

The sites that you would be working through are referred to as 'Outsourcing Sites'. They have a huge membership of providers (those doing the work) and people who want work done.

Below is a list of the most popular sites where you can get work, but again there are many others as well.

1. **Elance** - I love Elance for outsourcing my work, and on the flip side, for you, it could be a great way to make money online as a freelancer.

2. **oDesk** – Same as Elance, although many say that oDesk is the better choice for hiring programmers.

3. **Microworkers** – Make money by performing mini-tasks.

4. **MechanicalTurk** - Owned by Amazon, this site is similar to Microworkers, but maybe a bit more sophisticated.

5. **Fiverr** – Fiverr is quite different so make sure you read this, it is interesting. At Fiverr you can make money online by offering virtually any service or mini-task...the catch is you have to charge at least $5! When I say it is a catch, you have to make sure you offer something for $5 and you can add an upsell. Some get around this by offering a small service for $5 and say 'I can do ……… at $5 but if you want…….extra it would cost……' and that way they get a higher price for the more involved work they can do. Although in saying that, you would still have to keep prices low to be competitive. Have a look around at how providers write their gigs.

Fiverr is a site where you can list anything you like that you will offer)and which Fiverr will accept) to someone for the price of $5. A lot of people:

- sell SEO services (you need internet marketing knowledge for this)
- video reviews (you just need a webcam)
- sell things like sock puppets (you need the mad skills of making sock puppets)
- will friend you and pretend to be your girlfriend on Facebook for a few days (if you have a Facebook account and you're hot you can do this)
- review books
- sing happy birthday
- …or any number of silly things

Head over there and have a look around to see what people are offering. You will be amazed and I believe there will there is something you can be offering.

Like anything you try to do online you need to be very precise in how you word your 'gig' as they call the listing. Make sure you have a good graphic of the right size so that it shows well in the listing pages, something that will attract attention as buyers scroll through.

It's a no brainer, quick and if you get through the numbers, you will do very well. This is ideal for someone who can either, offer a product or service, mass produce it and sell a ton, or someone who needs some extra cash and is willing to offer whatever people need. But remember you will need to also promote your gigs to start getting work.

6.   Craigslist.com – this is another site a bit like Amazon, eBay, Etsy and Fiverr in that you can list anything (as long as it falls within the guidelines) and make money. Craigslist is more like Fiverr in that there are lots of different categories and lots of different things happening on the site.

•   You can sell things on Craigslist that you bought at a local tag sale or estate auction. Buy stuff in bulk on the cheap. Go to Craigslist and post it all. There is no posting fee, there is no selling fee (unlike selling through Ebay) and you always deal in cash with people on Craigslist. If you sell like this you should have a goal that for every $25 worth of goods you buy at a tag sale you should be able to sell them for at least $50 on Craigslist. In other words, make 100%. Hit up a few tag sales every weekend, post them on Craigslist and sell them and you can be making a spare couple hundred bucks a week

•   Do some work for people looking for skills that you have like writing, drawing, video recording, audio recording or whatever it is that you can do

•   You can work within your own language base which helps a lot of providers.

SELLING YOUR PHOTOS ONLINE (OR GRAPHICS)

There are several ways that a keen photographer can make money online.

Taking And Selling Your Own Photos On Your Own Website

This could mean selling in packages of 5 or 10 photos, or framed photos, a series of photos or any other way that you can think to promote your products through your own site. Also having your own site will mean that you will need to do lots of promoting.

If you go down this path of having your own site, check out my comments in 'Selling on your own site' further on, where I explain how you can make extra money from your own site than just with your own products. In your case you could be selling cameras, lenses, frames, etc. Make sure you read about that.

You might put together photo books, have them printed up on Createspace or a similar site and sell from your own site. You might do books from a specific holiday area and then promote those online to travelers, books on gardening, pets, flowers or anything that takes your fancy. This way you could sell from your site and also sell on a site like Amazon, Createspace, Kobo, Barnes and Noble, Nook, Lulu, etc. and this would give you several outlets from which to make your money.

These days it is so much easier to get books 'printed on demand' and this allows you to really sell yourself and your own products.

Selling Photos Through Online Royalty Free Sites

For a person who is very good at taking photos there are many sites that accept photos for on-selling. There seems to be no end to the types of photos you can upload. You can specialize or take whatever types of photos that the sites will accept and then upload them for selling.

The site will pay you a commission each time a member downloads one of the photos. It is the type of business where you can spend most of your time doing what you like, as in photography, and get paid an almost passive income once you have loaded up your work. You don't need to market your photos as the site looks after all that.

Most, if not all, of these same sites also accept graphics as well so if that is your forte you can make money with that as well or instead of.

To start with this method of making money, check out the sites, view their pictures and see what type of pictures are being downloaded a lot and that will give you an idea of the popular topics to work with.

Many of these sites promote 'free photos' but don't worry about that as it is just a means of getting viewers. They do have some free photos but they charge for most of their photos. There is a difference between 'free' photos which are just that – free – and royalty free photos which means that they can be used by the buyer for marketing and advertising etc., but which are paid for at the time of downloading.

Here is a list that you might like to investigate (there are lots more sites too):

- Fotolia http://fotolia.com/
- Dreamstime http://www.dreamstime.com/
- Photos http://photos.com/
- Stock.xchng http://www.sxc.hu/
- Shutterstock http://www.shutterstock.com/
- iStock http://www.istockphoto.com/
- Deposit Photos http://depositphotos.com/
- Stock Free Images http://www.stockfreeimages.com/
- Pixabay http://pixabay.com/
- Free Digital Photos http://www.freedigitalphotos.net/
- Public Domain Pictures http://www.publicdomainpictures.net/
- Morgue File http://morguefile.com/
- Every Stock Photo http://www.everystockphoto.com/

I have been downloading photos for about 6 years as do thousands of other website owners.

The idea is that people who work online need to add royalty free photos (Public Domain Free Photos) to their books, to their websites, to their articles, to training notes and the like and to do this they visit these photo sites to get their graphics. Not all the photos on these sites are royalty free and that is something that you would have to decide as the photographer.

SELLING YOUR OWN PRODUCTS ONLINE

This is a very interesting way to make money online but what most people do not realize is that not only can you make money online from selling your own products, but you can also earn money as an affiliate marketer. Read on and see how easy it is.

Maybe you make your own products, such as jewelry, t-shirts, hand painted shoes/glassware, wooden toys, photo books, etc. and wish to sell these online on your own site but make more money than you would just from your own products.

Selling on Your Own Site

If you sell through your own site it must be set up correctly so that the products are displayed properly and that you have a secure and well recognized payment gateway. With your own site you will have to put even more effort into marketing but at least you won't be competing against all the other 'shopkeepers' as you would on the larger sites.

Your site will need to have a payment gateway such as PayPal, Clickbank or one of the others, and you will have to set the site up in such a way that you can list products and update your listings at ease.

If you have your own site there are two ways that you can increase sales apart from just selling your own products:

Firstly: You can have a page that sells other products as an affiliate from say Amazon or eBay. What I mean is that say you make children's clothing and your partner makes wooden toys, you can have the same site selling both products. Because the site sells children's products, you can also have a page or pages, where you promote other children's items that are listed on say, Amazon. So you might have a page selling baby products (bottles, cots, etc.) and you may have a page selling electronic toys for toddlers. So you can build up quite an exciting site selling lots and lots of baby products, some of which you make and some that you will get paid a commission on. If you make jewelry you might have a couple of pages selling fashion items from Amazon or eBay, or if you make candles you might have some Amazon pages on your site selling party products or décor items.

You see the picture. It is a great way to grow your income, but again, it will need you to market them. You will need to become an Amazon Associate to be able to sell on your own site like this and you will be able to select the types of products that you want to sell.

Second: When you sell from your own site it is possible to set up your products to get affiliate sales (as opposed to being the affiliate). Clickbank is one of the main gateways for that purpose. Say you wrote information products, you can list them on Clickbank (and this is who you use as your payment gateway) and with strong promotion you can attract other online sellers to promote and sell your products at a commission. This helps in getting more names for your database and further sales.

When you have your own site you can have a page on Facebook and promote your products through that as well, which, if you build a strong following, can be very profitable. You can have your own page on Facebook whether you have your own site or have your products listed on one of the other larger sites, there is no restriction there, it is purely a method of social marketing.

If you need to set up a blog then you can get help from our ebook 'Setup A WordPress Website: one that works' from Amazon on Kindle: http://www.amazon.com/dp/B00CM1NASO

This will not tell you how to set up a selling site but you can try Storify.com or Prestashop.com to set up a professional selling site.

Selling Through Auction Sites and the Like

When you make products of your own you can sell them on your own website (as mentioned above) or on auction sites such as Amazon.com or eBay. Let me say at this point so that there is no misleading, if you decide to become a seller on these larger auction sites it pays to take some expert training as each site has its own idiosyncrasies and if you don't know the ins and outs of them you could spend a lot of hours without making any money.

Some of these sites like Amazon.com and eBay.com, where you would sell your products are auction sites, meaning you put your product up to receive bids from viewers but you can also set the price if you wish.

There are other sites like Etsy.com on which you can sell your products and have a set price that the viewers pay. These sites usually have a way for you to run an in-store sale or discount.

There are literally hundreds of sites like Etsy and you could research to find the one that would suit your product line as some of them specialize to a certain extent, in the product range they promote.

This book is about showing people some of the easier systems to start with so I make no apology about suggesting you get expert help. I always have got expert help, and will continue to do so as I work online. As I have mentioned before, there are so many ways to make money online that if you haven't been there, then don't waste countless hours learning by yourself. If you can afford it, pay to get the expert advice on any particular method that you want to pursue.

I currently am taking training about making money with ebooks even though I have been writing and selling ebooks for several years. I want to make more sales and I need to be shown how by someone who has been there and done it as I know want to expand my outlets for selling.

What needs to be taken into consideration when selling on these bigger sites is that if you sell through the bigger sites mentioned above you are competing with literally thousands of other members. Don't be fooled into thinking that you can rely on selling lots at that site just because you are on these popular sites. You will need to market your own products as well so that your products get recognition in the market place. As I said, starting out is always the hardest until you get a regular client base.

So depending on what it is that you would like to sell you would need to find the right selling site for you and that may not necessarily be the biggest and brightest site. You may find that you get better results on the smaller, less competitive sites, but you would still need to be responsible for your own marketing, although the site itself may do some.

AFFILIATE MARKETING

This is perhaps the most common or hottest way to make money online at the moment. You recommend a product, using an affiliate link. Someone clicks through that link, purchases the product and you get a commission. It's a simple concept, but sometimes difficult to execute. I have referred to this method of selling further back when talking about selling your own products online.

For years I avoided going too heavily into this concept even though I knew it to be profitable. I just could not get my head around it with everything else I was learning. But now it is actually one of the areas that I am concentrating on, with building my own affiliate sites with a view to building up a passive income. (I say passive but you do still need to actively market your site every now and then.)

One popular way to do affiliate marketing is to create a niche site (which is what I mentioned above that I am doing now), a site focused on one type of product and then populate the site with relevant articles which have affiliate links embedded. You could check out http://tipsfromtheinternet.com to view as an example where I actually have a lot of affiliate links but also a lot of articles.

Another way is to have your own site that has banners on, with affiliate links embedded. You write your blog about your chosen topic and have several relevant ads from which you can make money. This is an easy way to build up a number of sites, each on a different topic with a different set of banners. As long as you are doing some consistent marketing with article marketing, and social media you will eventually get monies from the site. Online marketers who go down this path have in the past had lots of sites, but more recently the trend has been to have one site with lots of pages and affiliate links throughout the site. The reason being, that when you have the one site you are building a site that is being recognized by the search engines as an authority site because it has so much information.

My site TipsFromtheInternet.com has been set up with this method in mind.

When online marketers have a lot of sites they are happy to get only a few hundred dollars from each site each month and that is why they have a large number of them. Once set up they really do not require much work, maybe about an hour a month, if that.

As for finding the products to work with the most important aspect is to make sure that you are linking to products that are best sellers and give the appearance of being around for some time.

Then when you have your site set up it is very important that you are using strong keywords when you are writing ads or articles.

Here are some good sources for products to sell as an affiliate:

1.   **Amazon Associates** – You need to sign up and become an Amazon Associate. How this works is when someone clicks on the affiliate link in your site, which could be embedded in text or in a graphic, they are taken through to the Amazon sales page of the product you have linked to. Amazon records the fact that you have sent someone to their site and you will receive a commission from anything they purchase within 24 hours.

Amazon.com is the biggest affiliate site and Amazon is such a well known site and has such a huge reach that you'll get a lot of people who click on your Amazon affiliate link but who happen to buy a different product and you will still get the credit for it.

(Below are other affiliate sites and they all work in a similar way.)

2.   **Commission Junction** – Huge marketplace of affiliate offers and very good products to choose from.

3.   **Clickbank** – One of the largest marketplaces for eBooks and other digital products

4.   **eBay** Partner Network – Earn a commission on eBay auctions that people find via your affiliate links.

When starting out in affiliate marketing take into consideration the length of time it will take you to get paid. Amazon will tally up your commissions for the current month but not pay you for another 60 days. That means that it could be 90 days from the sale until you get paid. Whereas Clickbank will pay every two weeks direct into your bank account.

The frequency of payments does make a difference when you are starting out.

TIP: when setting up your site
- make sure that the products that you choose are going to be good sellers (check sales figures) and it is best if they relate to the site you have, ie, a gardening site with gardening products, a dog information site with dog products, fashion site with fashion products
- that there is some sort of longevity to them in the market place as you don't want to have ads on your site that are not working any more

- that you check your site every now and then to make sure the ads are current and replace them if not.

If you need to set up a site and don't know how to, you can get an ebook of mine and a PDF on setting up your site:

Setup A WordPress WEBSITE – One That Works
http://www.amazon.com/dp/B00CM1NASO

There is a lot of hoo ha about affiliate sites because Google will not let you advertise affiliate links on their Pay Per Click (PPC) ads. Therefore as far as I and many other affiliate marketers are concerned, there is not much point in spending time adding lots of articles to your site to get Google rankings. The idea is to have a very simple site with 2-3 pages and then market it elsewhere to get the traffic. As a minimum use your social sites like Facebook, Twitter, Linkedin, Pinterest and others.

In saying that, there are lots of other places for PPC advertising, such as Yahoo, Facebook and Bing.

Your site does need to be optimized and does need to be attractive, but as far as having a lot of content regarding the products that now can be simplified by marketing your site yourself rather than waiting for Google to rank

SELLING PRODUCTS YOU DESIGNED, BUT DON'T OWN!

In some cases, you may want to design your own products (we're talking simple things, like t-shirts, magnets, mugs, etc.), but you don't want to take on the cost of having inventory that you can't sell, nor the cost of getting screens and so forth made up for screen printing and other such costs. There are sites which will print on demand and what you do is put up your design, decide what you want to put it on and then you can either sell your products from their site or you can have a site of your own.

The below options are great for this situation – for the most part, it's free to set up a virtual storefront, and you earn money when your products sell (and if nothing sells, it costs you nothing). I have not actually used this type of service but as an ex-retailer I can see lots of potential with this system.

These are generally great if you already have an established brand and want to sell your branded gear.

If you go down this path there is the possibility of big sales through companies and sports clubs, so make sure that you have a strong system for recording all sales and keeping names and contact details of all your buyers.

If you do want to market your products to companies and the like, make sure that your 'print on demand' company is putting out a top quality product.

1.   Cafe Press – You can easily have your own designs put on products like t-shirts, mugs, etc. and sell them from a virtual storefront through Cafe Press.

2.   Spreadshirt – Similar to Café Press but with T-Shirts only.

3.   Zazzle – Very similar to Cafe Press with a range of products.

4.   Shirt City – Another shirt design site/store.

A LIST OF TIPS FOR MAKING MONEY ONLINE

Here is a list of tips (in no particular order) that you need to be aware of to make money online:

1. A keyword is the word that people use to find products on the internet, either in a search engine like Google, Yahoo or Bing, but also within the search box on websites. It saves a lot of time when people are searching. Therefore if you are writing for the internet always be aware of using words that people would use to find your product, but don't overuse the word. About 3 times per hundred words is quite enough. And always use a keyword in any title or heading that you do.

2. If you have your own site then it is very important that you are using strong keywords when you are writing ads or articles, in fact in any form of marketing that you do, including when setting up your site.

3. When buying a domain name choose one that works with the niche you are working in and gives some idea of your business. In the past it was very important to try and put a keyword in your title to help with Google rankings but that is no longer critical, but what you should do is use a strong keyword in the tagline of your site (that is the second line of the header). Also use a keyword in your category titles if possible.

4. Use a good host for hosting your site such as Hostgator or GoDaddy. You don't want to put in a lot of work and have problems with your site crashing all the time. Hostgator offers hosting from about $3.95 a month.

5.   You need to accept the fact that you won't make money online unless you make a lot of noise! If working in outsourcing sites you need to put up lots of bids, if selling online you need to be actively marketing to get exposure. It is not the sort of job where you can work one hour this week and another hour in about two weeks with the hope of great results. Like any income earning source it takes time to develop.

6.   Marketing is really a whole other topic and very detailed at that, so if you decide to have your own site then I would suggest you take some marketing courses which would suit your style of business.

7.   Keep training yourself so that you are ahead of your competitors and be aware that things on the internet are changing on an almost daily basis so you need to keep up with that to keep earning well.

For more advanced ways of
MAKING MONEY ONLINE
simply type it into your browser.

http://homebusinesssuccessstrategies.net/advanced-online-income/

ANOTHER BOOK FROM MY HOME BASED
BUSINESS SERIES AVAILABLE AT
AMAZON KINDLE

HTTP://WWW.AMAZON.COM/DP/B00AW874LS

APPENDICES

Payment Gateways

Paypal.com   http://paypal.com

Clickbank.com   http://clickbank.com

Outsourcing Sites

Elance.com   http://elance.com

ODesk.com   http://odesk.com

Microworkers.com   http://mechanicalturk.com

Fiverr.com   http://fiverr.com

Craigslist.com   http://craigslist.com

Photo Listing Sites

Fotolia   http://fotolia.com

Dreamstime   http://www.dreamstime.com/

Photos http://photos.com /

Stock.xchng http://www.sxc.hu/

Shutterstock http://www.shutterstock.com/

iStock http://www.istockphoto.com/

Deposit Photos http://depositphotos.com/

Stock Free Images http://www.stockfreeimages.com/

Pixabay http://pixabay.com/

Free Digital Photos http://www.freedigitalphotos.net/

Public   Domain   Pictures
http://www.publicdomainpictures.net/

Morgue File   http://morguefile.com/

Every Stock Photo   http://www.everystockphoto.com/

Affiliate Sites

Amazon.com   http://amazon.com

Kaye Dennan

Clickbank.com http://clickbank.com
CommissionJunction.com http://commissionjunction.com

Social Media Sites
Facebook.com   http://facebook.com
Twitter.com   http://twitter.com
LinkedIn.com   http://linkedin.com
Pinterest.com   http://pinterest.com

Reputable Trainers or Resources
HomeBusinessSuccessIdeas.com
          http://homebusinesssuccessideas.com
NicheProfitClassroom.com
          https://imi.infusionsoft.com/go/bonus/a25874
MichelleShaeffer.com   http://michelleshaeffer.com
DecisiveMinds.com   http://decisiveminds.com
KathleenGage.com   http://kathleengage.com

Other Books By Kaye Dennan Available From Her Amazon Author Page

http://www.amazon.com/-/e/B00AVQ6KKM

ABOUT THE AUTHOR

Kaye Dennan has a background in small business and for the past 7 years has been working online full-time, building websites and marketing her own and affiliate products.

Kaye is committed to helping others make money online and building up a business that they can work from home. This book covers some very simple ways to make money online and as is spoken about during the book, once the basics are learned time can be put into the more complex techniques.